The Old Man and The New Man

By Ray Berto

PRESS

TABLE OF CONTENTS

2 Corinthians 5:17 says, "Therefore, if any man be in Christ, he is a new creature; old things are passed away; behold, all things are become new."

M y name is Ray and this is my story. I can't remember all of the events of my life, but I've included what I can remember that I think will be of importance. It's difficult to write this book because I don't like my past or the hurt and pain I went through. I would like to lock it away and just forget it. But, if by writing this book, I can lead someone else into truth, keep someone from making the same mistakes I did, or hold out a ray of hope to someone, it is well worth it. John 14:6 says, "Jesus saith unto him, I am the way, the truth, and the life: no man cometh unto the Father, but by me."

It is my prayer that your heart will be touched with God's love and healing power and that your mind will truly grasp what a wonderful God I have and what a wonderful God you can have. Open your heart to Him as you read my story.

Note: The names have been changed to protect the real people.

Chapter One

Childhood

For all of my life, my dad was an alcoholic. I could not "preach" to him, take him to church or talk to him about religion in any way. I could only place him in the hands of Jesus.

Most of my childhood memories of my dad are not very pleasant. We lived by a tavern and I remember my dad coming home mean and drunk. In his drunken state, he was often abusive.

He once threw a light bulb into the eyes of my older sister. I'm thankful it didn't damage her eyes. My older brother, Bob, was thrown into an iron crib which resulted in a permanent facial injury. I had hot gravy thrown in my face when I was about a year old. I still have a scar under my left eye. There were many other incidents of violence at the hands of my dad.

My mom tried to protect us from my dad, but he would beat her and push her around, too. She always took us to the doctor to be sure we hadn't suffered any serious injuries from my father, but she couldn't stop him.

My mom knew it was the alcohol that made him act abusive. So, one day she dumped all of his beer out of the bottles in the back yard. When he came home drunk and looking for his beer, he became enraged when he found she had poured it all out. As children, we were always frightened when dad was drunk and angry, so we began to cry. This seemed to anger him all the more and he started to come after us. My mom stepped in between and he pushed her and caused her to fall and chip her ankle bone.

Not only was my father abusive and alcoholic, but he was not a provider. He spent most of his money on alcohol; not food or the necessities we needed as a family. Our relatives brought us food and clothes. My uncle and my grandfather brought us food one day and told my dad to leave it alone, it was for the kids. My dad got angry and started a fight. My sister, brother and I watched as my uncle and grandfather walked away leaving my dad in a pool of blood. My older sister took us into the bedroom and we crawled under the bed. This was our "safe" place and she would always put her hand over our mouths and tell us to be quiet because daddy was home and he'd beat us.

Though my mom tried to protect us, all of us, including herself, were still being abused by my dad. For some reason, she wouldn't leave him. For a while we lived in an old trailer of my grandfather's on his property. I remember my mother getting up in the middle of the night and stepping on a rat. It was while we were living in this trailer that my relatives turned my mom into the authorities and they removed all three of us and put us in foster homes. I was only four years old at the time, but I remember all of us kicking, biting and screaming to go back to our mom. They put my sister in a different home than my brother and myself.

Losing us kids was a terrible ordeal for my mom. She wouldn't eat and finally got so sick she was almost hospitalized. She went to a kind doctor that told her that not eating was not an answer. He explained that if something happened to her, we would be without a mother. This seemed to give her the determination she needed and she began to eat. She still had problems sleeping and I know she spent a lot of time walking the floor and crying.

The foster home that my sister stayed in had another girl about the same age. Every time the other girl did something wrong, my sister got blamed. My sister would then have to pull her pants down and bend over the bathtub and get spanked with a belt. She felt angry, hurt and humiliated.

My brother and I had to work in the garden where we lived. We were not allowed to play with our trucks and cars in the house; we would get spanked if we did. We didn't get to see my sister or my mom very often. It was a very painful and lonely time.

One time, I remember my mom coming to see us and she brought us some toys. When we saw her we ran out of the house and said, "Hi Lila!" It hurt her terribly that we called her by her name instead of calling her "mom."

We were in foster homes for two years. During this time period, my mom and dad got a divorce. When we got to go home and live with our mom again, we were thrilled. We were all together and dad wasn't there to abuse us. We were relieved that this ordeal was over and happy to be together again.

I don't remember this period of my life very well because I was so young. I do know that my mom got married again. This marriage lasted one year. I also remember that we didn't seem to have very much. All we had for school clothes were two shirts, one pair of pants and a pair of shoes. We ate a lot of hamburger over rice and pork-n-beans.

Mom's second marriage also gave us another sister. Our step-dad did everything he could for his new daughter, but he wouldn't do anything for the rest of us. Again, we were being abused. I remember one time he hit my brother Bob over the head with a glass gallon jug. I remember getting hit with a hammer by my step-dad's brother. By 1962, my older sister had been through enough so she got married and moved to California.

The house we were living in was torn in half by a twister. The contents of all of the cupboards were falling out onto the floor and breaking. Fortunately, the only injury was a bump on the head from a coffee pot. From this house, we moved to a crowded one-room cabin. Mom had to do all of the cooking on a wood stove. We took our baths outside in the washtub.

It seems like one of us was always having an accident. My brother was constantly getting stitches. My sister cut her foot with an ax while cutting fire wood for the stove. I broke my wrist and knocked my elbow out of place when I fell from a tree. Though these were just childhood accidents, they were stressful to my mom.

My mom has restless, because we moved a lot. We lived in Algona, WA, then Redmond, WA, then back to Algona. The second time we lived in

Algona, WA, we lived there for about three years. I was in the second grade at the time. However, my school experiences were less than stellar. I began skipping school, fighting, smoking and eventually joined a gang called the Swamp Foxes. The gang didn't last, but my troubled ways did. One of the only positive things I remember about school was coming in 2nd at our school track meet.

I really wasn't supervised. I ran around, and did exactly as I pleased. I had a terrible temper and if I didn't get my way, I would really get mad. My language was poor, I began stealing small things and my friends were a pretty wild bunch. I was always in trouble in the classroom. I ended up in the principal's office more than once. I threw erasers at the girls, put tacks on the classroom chairs and caused trouble any way I could. Just for the sport of causing trouble.

I always felt picked on, so I wanted to align with others kids to fit in. Then as a group, we would pick on other kids.

It was about second grade when my step-dad molested my brother and I.

I don't know who called the police, but they came out and took us to the Police Station to ask us questions about what happened. It was very scary. We were afraid that our step-dad would hurt us for telling on him. I was told that when he found out we went to the police, he left the state. It took us a long time to stop being afraid. We always feared he would come back and hurt us. Fortunately, we didn't see him again until we were teenagers. We later found out that he spent four years in jail. It seems he had molested others as well.

Between 5th grade and eighth grade, we moved several times back and forth between Woodinville, Algona and Auburn. It was during 8th grade that I took an interest in wrestling. The coach offered to pay my way so I could join the wrestling team, but I refused. I didn't want any handouts. I was just plain tired. Tired of moving, tired of trying to make new friends. I adopted an "I don't care" attitude about everything. By this time we had moved 20 times, if not more. I was tired and I was angry.

With no dad, there was no one to teach me how to work on a car, play sports, camp, fish, etc. My mom tried to be both mom and dad. I know she loved us and she tried to discipline us. But by this time, I paid no attention to her. I didn't even listen.

Chapter Two

Teen Years

S ometime during junior high school, I began to notice girls. And I liked what I saw. In my search for identity and a sense of belonging, I joined a club called, "The Family." There were about 50 members at the time. We wore jeans, t-shirts, beetle boots (or motorcycle boots) and long hair. I was drinking, taking drugs, sniffing glue, and lusting after girls. I still held onto my "tough" attitude which lead to a lot of fighting. It didn't take much to start a fight with me because of the temper I had.

We used to hide cigarettes by a big tree not far from the school and go there for a smoke during lunch time. We sneaked whiskey into the school restrooms, threw water balloons down the hallways at the students and teachers. Sometimes we would run by a classroom and throw in a water balloon as we went by. We played cruel pranks on new students. I was acting the pain and frustration I felt inside. But it didn't stop.

I got kicked out of P.E. with two others for a week because we were horse-playing instead of listening to the teacher. We had to clean up the school grounds. I was kicked off the school bus for the remainder of the year for fighting.

I was finally kicked out of junior high for the rest of the year for hitting a teacher. I felt that the teacher picked on me and I told him so. He pinched my shoulder so I spun around and hit him in the mouth. I really had a chip on my shoulder.

Two other guys and myself broke into a laundromat. We were looking for money, but we didn't get anything. We heard someone coming and took off. We didn't realize it at the time, but this person had called the police. The police caught us and after the people at the small laundromat identified us, they took us to the Police Station. I was sixteen at the time. Looking back, the judge was good to me. He said if I didn't get into any more trouble for a year, he would remove this offense from my record. I had been living with my sister and brother-in-law, but was afraid of what my brother-in-law would do if he found out about the arrest. So, I gave my Aunt's phone number. When they called her, she told them she didn't know me! I finally had to tell the police I was staying with my sister and her husband. They came and took me home. The minute we got into the house, my brother-in-law started yelling at me and pushing and slapping me. I finally went to bed crying. I was so scared of what had happened. All I really wanted was for someone to care about me. I would have been glad if they had grounded me or given me chores, but to shout and hit me was just more of what I'd already experienced. And that didn't mean love to me.

My mom was worried about me. I had been staying at a friend's place. The police felt she should know where I was, so they told her where I was staying. She felt more at ease knowing.

I had a friend whose family let me live with them for a while. Before they would let me move in, they wanted my mom's approval. My mom approved and I moved in. This family was Catholic and I remember going to church with them for the year I lived there. I worked with my friend's dad for room and board. He was the janitor at the church.

This was a good year, and I enjoyed the sense of family I felt in this home. One night I went out with a couple of friends and got so drunk, I could barely walk. A friend delivered me to the front door and left. I tried to get into bed without waking anyone. I took three steps down the stairs to the basement and fell the rest of the way. On the way down, I grabbed a shelf which was full of home canned goods and several of them broke. I hit my head on an aluminum ladder. I crawled from there to bed. The next morning, my friend's parents were waiting for me in the kitchen.

They had already cleaned up my mess and I didn't even remember the incident. However, they did. They told me everything I did. They didn't yell or hit me. They talked to me and asked me how I felt about what happened. For once in my life I felt wanted and loved. Someone really cared for me and cared about what happened to me. I was overwhelmed that someone actually cared enough to discipline with love. I was put on restriction for two weeks and had to do extra chores.

One time I went to a party and got so drunk that I passed out in the parking lot. Friends carried me to their apartment.

Once a friend and I went to a drive-in with a couple of other guys that we had just met. We also brought a couple cases of beer and paid our way into the movie. We had the money, but no car. They let us in anyway. After the movie, the people we met drove us to a gas station that was close to my friend's house.

We climbed into the back of a U-Haul truck to get out of the cold and rain. My friend sneaked me into his house and grabbed a couple of sleeping bags. The next morning, we went over to another friend's house. No one was up, so we sat on the front steps. His mom and dad were driving around looking for him and had seen him sitting there. They stopped, picked him up and took him home. I went in and took off my jacket and my t-shirt was all brown. I had gotten sick and hadn't even remembered. My friend went back to the U-haul truck to get his sleeping bags, but they were gone. So was the truck.

I also remember when my friends and I would go down to the river and have parties. I remember one time when a runaway [whom the police were looking for] stayed with us. We hid him until he finally went home.

We also used to race cars. One time this car blew a tire on a back street and went sliding into a telephone pole onto its right side. It was a 2-door Buick and when it hit the right side of the car, it became a 3 door. The car was totaled. Fortunately, I was not in that car. The driver received 17 stitches on his forehead and was knocked out. Two other people went flying out of the back window. One skidded down the road on his rear end right into a ditch. The other went flying up on some tracks. All of these guys were treated and released. A girl that was sitting on the side that was caved in, had her hair caught on a piece of the car. When the car was tossed around and around, about 100-150 feet down the road, she was drug under it.

An ambulance took her to the hospital. She was fine until she got inside the hospital, then she went into shock. She had to learn how to walk all over again. The police asked us if we were racing. We told them we weren't. He said we had to have been, because of the nature of the accident. He said this kind of accident couldn't happen unless we had been racing. We stuck to our story, because before the police came, we made a pact together. The girl was in the hospital for about two months, and is now walking again. I'll never forget what she told us.

"I died under that car and saw God," she said. "I told Him that I promised I would never get into trouble again."

I hope she kept her promise, I haven't seen her since.

The drugs that I took at this time were pot, crystal (It's a white powder that you mix in a glass of water), German hash, and speed. We would put Alka Seltzer in coke, take aspirin, and put sage and tobacco together to get high. Once a friend of mine and myself tried tea leaves, but it only made us sick. I stopped sniffing glue when I found out that it eats your brain. When a friend of mine would get mad, he'd hit a wall, which had a steel plate behind it. Consequently, he broke his knuckles. I stopped taking speed after I broke out in a cold sweat and got dizzy. I had to leave work. I only tried crystal once. I eased up on drugs a little until I was only using pot and hash. I stopped taking the German hash after my cousin and I tried walking down a street and couldn't walk in a straight line. A police car was coming down the road so my cousin bent down and pretended to tie his shoe. I leaned up against a fence. We waited for the police car to disappear before we started off.

My house in Auburn, WA was about two to three blocks down the road. My cousin came over to visit. She would stop by the police station because her husband was a policeman. They asked her what she was up to. She told them she was visiting her cousin just down the road. They pointed out the house and asked her if that was where her cousin lived. I later found out that one of my aunts turned me in for drugs, beer and parties. I never was arrested.

Once a friend of mine and myself hitchhiked down to Portland, OR. We were going to California. A guy picked us up, bought us some beer and a motel room for the night. He later asked me what I was doing with that type of a friend. He then encouraged me to go back home and make something of myself. The next day, I went home and never saw that friend again.

Another time, a cousin and I were hitchhiking to Great Falls, Montana. It was snowing and very cold. We made it to Ellensburg where a state trooper picked us up for hitchhiking on the freeway. We weren't really on the freeway, we were on an exit ramp. The trooper took us to the nearest

Sheriff's office. He told the sheriff that we were hiking on the freeway. I explained that we were actually on the exit ramp. The sheriff started laughing at the trooper because he was getting mad at me and I wasn't about to change my story. The trooper said that if he caught us hanging around there again, he'd pick us up for vagrancy. We told the sheriff's department that we didn't have a place to sleep or any money. They put us up in a cell and gave us coffee and a meal. Then they took us on a tour of the jail. They showed us the bad guys and the meanest guy they had in jail. They also showed us the solitary room. After showing us around, they gave us a cell with soft mattresses and a shower. The shower even came with a wash cloth and soap. That night we went right to sleep. My cousin called his dad and he sent us money for a bus ticket. My uncle told my cousin that he didn't have enough money to buy two tickets. He said for me to ask if some nearby truckers were going to Auburn and would let me ride along. I finally found a truck that was carrying some chickens. The next ride was with a drunk in a station wagon. The final ride was with six army guys. I remember one of them saying, "don't worry if he tries anything—there's only one of him and six of us." I couldn't wait to get out of there. It took me awhile to get over the fear of that trip home. All of my personal belongings went with my cousin. I never heard from him again.

I was a teenager with a very big mouth. I'd back talk adults and my mother. There were times when I should've been beaten up, put in jail, or even dead. But, the grace of God protected me during that time and I didn't even realize it. Sure I got into fights and would get black eyes, a bloody nose, cut lips, etc., but nothing really serious. I remember one guy that would stop me after school and tease me. This went on for weeks until I had finally had enough. I threw my books down and said, "OK, if you want to fight, let's fight!" Instead of fighting, we became real good friends.

There was another guy I knew who was going with the same girl that I was, but neither of us knew about the other. One day we both went to her house. We asked her to come outside in the pouring rain and decide which one she wanted. She said, "I want you both." Eventually, my friend won and I lost. I also remember another girl that I was dating. She was about thirteen or fourteen and I was about sixteen or seventeen. Her dad chased me off and said if he ever found me around her again, he'd stomp me into the ground. He was an alcoholic. We would sneak around to see each other. One day she asked me if I would drive her and her mom away from her dad. I wouldn't and we broke up.

My mom moved back to Auburn just before my senior year of high school. I had only one year to go but I dropped out of school. I had one teacher that picked on me all the time. I finally got fed up and threw my book and walked out. I started going with this girl just before I dropped out of school. She was going with another guy which I didn't know. I found out about the other guy when she told me she was pregnant by him. She was about four months along. He didn't want her and told me that if I wanted her I could have her. I felt sorry for her and this was the first time I had any kind of sexual relationship with a girl.

Chapter Three

Marriage

Marriage is something neither of us was prepared for. She was sixteen and I was twenty. I had planned to get a job before we got married so I could support my wife, but her dad didn't want us to wait because of the pregnancy. We felt forced into marriage before we were ready. I was unemployed, smoking, drinking and on welfare. Our first home was a one-bedroom apartment. Family and friends pitched in to help us with the rent. Our only transportation was a car that my wife's brother gave us as a wedding present.

I decided to settle down and be a good husband and, soon, father. We had a little boy named Marty and soon after, my wife was pregnant with our second child. Our daughter was born in December. In two years our third child was born and in two more years our fourth child was born. We now had two boys and two girls.

We no longer fit a one-bedroom apartment, so we moved into a duplex. I was working now, but much of our life was partying. We went all out. We bought booze, snacks and provided the place for the parties. Our guests brought even more booze and we partied all night long. We drank, danced and played loud music. At this time, our marriage started to crumble.

My wife began babysitting for one of the couples we were friends with. They were moving and needed someone to watch the kids. It wasn't long before I knew something was wrong. I was staying at home watching our children and waiting for her to come home. When she came in late, I exploded. She finally confirmed that she was seeing someone else.

We stayed together, but I was suspicious and wouldn't let her go anywhere without me. We continued to have wild parties. I thought things were going okay and then I came home from work one day to an empty house. My wife, kids, furniture and everything else that wasn't a personal possession of mine, was gone. I knew she was probably with the guy she was seeing because I could tell her car had been at his place. The car leaked oil badly. I found a note from my wife that said, "Don't bother looking for me, because you won't find me and I'm not coming back." I took the note and went to see her dad. Together, her dad and I began to look for her. I had only been to this guy's house once for a party, but we finally found it. I parked in the driveway and my father-in-law told me to stay in the car. He went up to the door and asked for his daughter. She came to the door. He told her to get the kids and to get into the car.

We were all in the car on the way home and my wife looked at me and yelled, "I hate you!" "I don't love you, why did you come looking for me?" Her dad told her to be quiet. He also told her that it wouldn't do any good for her to leave me because she didn't have any place to go.

My brother-in-law and I went to get all of our furniture and other belongings. I had my family and furniture back, but the marriage was still in desperate trouble. Instead of working on the relationship, I would leave and go the tavern and get drunk. I wasn't trying to hurt her, I was hurting inside myself.

One night I was out drinking and I had left her a note telling her that I didn't want to be married. Her dad and brother came looking for me that night. My father-in-law took me outside and told me that if I ever bothered his daughter again, I'd have to have the police department stop him from coming after me. Her brother said that he'd finish me off if his dad didn't. They left, and my wife and I talked and decided we'd try once more to make a go of our marriage. I was in a low paying job, so we applied for low-income housing and got approved. We moved into a three-bedroom house.

I tried to spend as much time as I could with my kids as they were growing up. I played with them, taught them to clean their rooms, how to dress themselves and how to get along with each other. I changed and dressed the little ones. I also did a lot of the house cleaning and some of the cooking. But, hard as we tried, the marriage still failed when our fourth child was still a baby.

In looking back, I can see why this marriage didn't work. First, I became unemployed when my job site burned to the ground. Secondly, my wife was having an affair with my brother-in-law. It had been going on for some time. When I left for work, he would come to my house and see my wife. The man's wife eventually forced my wife to tell me what was going on. I was outraged. When I asked her why, she couldn't tell me. I told her I was going to move out and she bent down and grabbed my leg and cried, begging me not to leave. But, I was too mad. I just walked out the door.

I found a one-bedroom cabin and went back to get my belongings. My brother-in-law came while I was there and asked me to stay and work it out with my wife. He said he was sorry. I wanted to hit him in the face, but it wouldn't have proved anything. We had been close friends at one time. We fished and camped together, even lent each other money. I couldn't understand how he could do this to me. He gave the same answer my wife did, "It just happened." He apologized again and left. I packed up my belongings and left.

About a month later, my wife and kids paid me a visit. She told me that she had no where to live. I let her move in with me. I was still angry. We weren't getting along, but I wanted to try. I was drinking, angry, and I didn't treat her very well.

My wife tried to fix me up with other women, and she dated other men. Her dad found out she was on a date with another man and he got a little crazy. He went and got her. Then they went to his house and talked about our problem. The next thing I knew a van pulled up in front of our house and several people jumped out. They began to tear pictures off the walls, packing everything in sight and moving everything they could move. I even had one of our kids taken right out of my arms. I knew at this point that it was really over.

We divorced and I began partying and drinking to hide my sadness. I had trouble holding a job. Once, I almost got fired for drinking on the job and another job I quit before they could fire me for drinking on the job. I went from job to job and lived from place to place. I slept in cars and friend's houses, I didn't even have a permanent address. A part of me even felt they would be better off without me. My divorce papers said I had visitation rights, but I really didn't force the issue because of my lifestyle.

I didn't see my kids again for quite some time. I met a pregnant girl at a tavern and began to date her. We later got married. We would go out and drink and party until the bars closed and even after the bars closed sometimes. When the baby was born, I wanted to stay home more. We both drank and my wife smoked pot. When our daughter was a little older, we enrolled her in a day care school in Auburn at Calvary Temple Church. The people were really nice and friendly and our little girl loved the church. My wife worked in the daytime and I worked at night. Every payday, I would take our daughter, Annie to see her mom at lunch time. Then, I would take her to day care on my way to work. I had the opportunity to really get to know my daughter during the days I spent with her. We went to the park, went for walks, we went to the store, and I walked along side as she rode her bike. My wife got upset because our little girl was getting so attached to me and paid little attention to her mother. My wife accused her of becoming a "daddy's girl." I was still drinking, but less than usual. We moved into a nicer place, and had a little one in day care and I thought she was more important. I was building my whole life around her because she meant so much to me. We didn't have a lot of money at the time, so I told my wife we should quit drinking so much and stay home. I wanted to watch how we spent our money. But, she was hooked on alcohol and couldn't stop.

I was unaware at the time, but she was making passes at my friends. When I found out, I was furious. I pulled one guy out of my wife's car and started beating on him. We left the bar at closing that night, went home, and began to argue. Finally, I laid down on the carpet with a blanket and pillow and pretended I was asleep. She took our daughter and left. I waited until she left, then I got into my car and started looking for her. I went over to the home of the guy she was seeing and there she was. When she saw me, she took off again. I followed and almost forced her off the road before she stopped. I went to the passenger door of her car and he was down on the floorboard holding onto the seat. I grabbed him and started beating on him. As my wife and I left him there, he was yelling, "your wife has a problem." That problem was drinking and sex. She wouldn't make love with me. But she made love with others. She even had an open relationship with a known lesbian. She spent a lot of time in bars with her. When she and my wife and I went out, my wife and I would fight and I would end up sleeping on the couch while they shared our bed. I did see them kiss one time while their arms were wrapped around each other. At the same time I had a friend that hung around our house a lot. We would get a babysitter and the four of us would go out. When I took the babysitter home later, the three of them would stay at my house and have a threesome. It was becoming increasingly uncomfortable to have both of these friends around our house all the time. I asked my friend one time if he thought my wife and her friend made love and he said, "I know they do." When I asked him how he knew, he wouldn't tell me, but said he had his ways of knowing.

My wife was smoking pot and drinking heavily. I couldn't understand why she was doing these things. She wasn't like this when we got married. It finally got to the point where she was selling our possessions to get money for alcohol. She left the house one time to sell something so she could buy diapers for our little girl. When she didn't arrive back home for a long time, I started calling her favorite bars and, sure enough, found her drinking. I put a towel on my daughter instead of a diaper. I called the bar several more times before I finally got my wife to come home.

Shortly after this incident, my wife lost her job. Her employer had a party for all those that were laid off and she went. I found out that she and one of the men at the party were kissing, and eventually began to date. This began a big change in my wife. She began taking our little one with her while she hunted for a job. The other thing that happened at this time was that she wouldn't let me touch her. When I asked her if she was seeing another man, she denied it. But, the man's girlfriend called me and told me that my wife and this man were having an affair. The man's girlfriend had questioned him and he admitted he was having an affair and told her it was my wife he was involved with. She also told me that when my wife said she was out looking for work, she was actually meeting her boyfriend in hotels and motels. I thanked this woman for the information and told her I would take care of things.

When my wife got home, I asked her how "he" was? She said, "Who?" I told her she knew who I was talking about. She continued to deny it. Finally, I told her about his girlfriend calling. As we were talking, the man's girlfriend called again and asked to talk to my wife. My wife refused to talk with her but yelled "Thanks a lot!" loud enough for her to hear. After I hung up, my wife and I got in a fight and were yelling at each other. She grabbed our youngest little girl and headed out the door yelling, "you can't even afford to put gas in your own car." I said a lot of things to her and even called her names. I'm sure not proud of myself for what I said. I didn't know what to do. I called my mom, but she wasn't any help. I remember feeling very lonely. It wasn't long before we separated and eventually divorced.

It was right before my wife left that I became a Christian. I was so hurt over the marriage problems and I didn't know what to do. So I went to Calvary Temple Church in Auburn, WA. It took three times of going to the altar for prayer before I really felt I was a Christian. I didn't understand at the time that it was the Holy Spirit who kept drawing me to Jesus. It was Satan trying to pull me away. I am so thankful the Lord didn't give up on me and that He won the fight for my life. When my wife left, I remember laying on our bed and praying and crying for the Lord to take all of the evil out of the house and out of me. He did! As I was praying, I tossed around on the bed and this ball of fire came out of me and faded away and then the whole room lit up. During all of this, I wasn't afraid. I knew the Lord was there and I felt warm, comfortable and ministered to by His Spirit.

After the second divorce, my cousin and older brother moved in with me. It was a struggle to keep the bills paid. My cousin wasn't working at all and my older brother was only getting $300.00 a month. I was working, but half of my paycheck was being paid out in child support payments for the children from my marriage. After a short time, we moved into a two bedroom house. The street we moved on was called party street and I'm sorry to say, I started partying all over again. After two months of drinking and partying, my older brother and myself moved out into a two bedroom apartment in Kent, WA. I started dating a girl who had a little boy. Soon, my brother moved out and the girl moved in. After only a month, I told her I couldn't live with her because I wanted to live for God. I moved in with my mom for a short time, until my brother and I got a two bedroom apartment in Fife, Washington.

Though I was trying to live for God, I had another affair with a girl that lived next door to us. I was so upset that I had failed. I apologized to her and told her I was wrong to have slept with her.

One night my cousin and friend were out drinking and I heard this voice calling my name saying, "Ray! Ray! What are you doing? You've been saved." I asked everyone around me if they called my name and they said they hadn't, and that I must be crazy. I looked all around me and there was no one around. After that night, I went home and got on my knees and cried to the Lord and asked for forgiveness. I began to change. My cousin even noticed how much better I got along with my brother. When he asked me what happened, I told him about the Lord and gave him a Bible to read.

After a couple of months, my older brother and I moved out into a two bedroom apartment in Kent, Washington. I started dating a girl with a small son. Soon, she moved in with me and my brother moved out. I knew within just a few weeks that I could not continue to live this way. I knew I wanted to live for God and I couldn't continue to live with her. She helped me move into my mother's house. Eventually, my brother and I moved into an apartment in Fife.

Our next door neighbor was a girl with two small children. I dated her once and then spent the night at her house. I never felt so sick in all my life. I apologized to her and told her that I was wrong and that I wanted to serve God.

In a month or two, I once again found myself at my mother's house. My brother moved out again and I couldn't afford the apartment on my own. It had only been a year since I asked Jesus to be the Lord and Savior of my life. As you can see, I had my ups and downs; I often stumbled and fell with my Christian walk. I prayed, and wanted to serve God, but I still lived in the world. I prayed, but I didn't listen to what the Lord said to me. Even though, I was really struggling, the Lord never left me. He carried me along and forgave me for every one of the sins I committed. I was a new Christian and I wasn't even sure what to do. I soon developed the pattern of going to work and after work was over I would go home and just sit in my bedroom and pray and read the Bible.

My older brother thought I was taking it "too far." He felt I was locking myself in my bedroom and locking the world outside. He said I would have to come out and face life sometime. But, I not only loved God, I feared him and I didn't want to sin anymore. I wanted to be sure I would go to heaven and not to hell. I was sure I'd go to hell that first year I was a Christian because I had failed so many times. So, I continued to retreat to my bedroom and listen to Christian music and to biblical teaching, and to pray. During this time, I read the Bible through about three or four times. I wanted to shine for God—I wanted everyone to see that there was something different in my life. I spent about two years out in that bedroom in the garage. I prayed at mealtimes, thanking God for the food and everything else he provided for me. God knew my needs and when I prayed and asked Him to meet them, He would provide. I can't blame anyone else for the way I lived.

I made my own choices. I finally made a choice to live in this world, but to serve God. 1 John 1:9 says, "If we confess our sins, He is faithful and just to forgive us our sins, and to cleanse us from all unrighteousness." When I was at my mom's home, I was growing closer and closer to the Lord. I wanted to learn all I could about the Lord.

I wanted to see my kids again. I knew that I would have to do what my ex-wife told me to do. In the past, my step-dad had talked dirty around the kids and my ex-wife got really mad. Even though I tried to explain, it didn't make any difference. I did get them one time and we watched a true story about how babies were born, but that made her upset too. I knew that I would have to watch what we did when I had the kids so she would continue to let me see them.

During that two years I grew in the Lord, I tried several different denominations. But, everyone had a different interpretation of God's Word and I just got confused. It seemed like each denomination was right and they thought all the others were wrong. It was as if each denomination made a different set of "rules" that must be followed or you weren't a good Christian. I finally got to the point where I didn't want any part of "religion." I still wanted God, but I wanted Him to lead me, guide me, give me understanding and knowledge, including leading me to a church that taught the Bible as the only Word of God. I did learn one thing during my search and that is what really matters is that the true gospel is preached so that people get saved. John 3:16 says, "For God so loved the world, that He gave His only begotten Son, that whosoever believeth in Him should not perish, but have everlasting life."

After a lot of searching, God lead me to Milton Assembly of God Church. The pastor, his wife, and the congregation made me feel loved, accepted, wanted, and the church believed in the Holy Spirit.

I told my first wife what had happened to me since I asked Jesus into my heart. She said that was good for me, but she wasn't interested for herself. My second wife said that I couldn't afford to put gas in my truck, so Jesus didn't really provide.

For about 7½ years I lived by myself. I was single and had no girlfriend during this time. It was just God and me. I lost two friends in horrible accidents, but God brought me His peace. The Holy Spirit ministered to me all the time. I was never alone, and I really learned a lot.

At this time, I had a job in Kent, Washington. One part of my job was to drive the forklift to empty the dumpsters in the factory. There was a girl who would smile and wave at me every time I went by. I found out she asked her supervisor if I was married or single. When I would leave at night, she would smile and wave at me. This went on for quite a while. Then one day when I was going by on the forklift, she stopped me and asked me how my weekend was. I told her I had worked that weekend and that I didn't like working Sundays, but I needed the money. I told her I felt Sunday was God's day and I wanted to be in church. I asked her if she would like to go to the play, Jesus of Nazareth. She agreed and asked if her girlfriend could accompany us. I also took my mom and my nephew. We were all blessed! We dated, went to church together. One Sunday in church, the pastor asked who wanted to find a Christian mate. She and I both stood up.

We went for walks and talked. I told her about my marriages, my four kids, my child support payments, and that I didn't make much money. I asked her if she could accept my children. She said, "Yes." We were both looking for someone to live for God with. We desired to pray, worship, share and read the Bible together. I prayed and asked God to guide us and give us His wisdom on whether or not we should get married. She was praying also. Soon after, we went to Ocean

Shores and I proposed and she accepted! When we got home I took her to my mom's and introduced her as mom's new daughter-in-law. Then I took her into the kitchen, sat her down, knelt on one knee and proposed again...and she accepted again. I wanted to be sure I had done it properly. When people found out we were getting married, they asked us what made us decide to get married. Our answer was that it was the air from the salt water in the ocean. That kept them guessing!

I thanked God for this girl and gave Him the praise and glory for her. On the day of our wedding, I was driving along singing and praising God and getting on the exit to the freeway. I checked behind me to see if anything was coming. When I looked in front of me again, all I could see was the tail lights of a big semi-truck. I slammed on my brakes and spun completely around, landing on the shoulder of the road heading the opposite way. I sat for a moment and thanked God for watching over me, then I turned the car around and went home. I called Karen and she said I would need to pick her and her maid of honor up because her car wouldn't start. I told her what happened to me and she didn't believe me at first. We decided that the devil didn't want us to get married. But, we did. We spent one night in a hotel and had to go back to work the next day. We rented an apartment and began married life. We knew it would take some time to get used to each other and for her to get to know my children. It was really rough at first. We both had expectations and neither of us was meeting the expectations of the other. Accepting my kids was more difficult for my wife, too, because she can't have children of her own and she felt the pain of that. We prayed that God would work a miracle and that she would have a baby. Eventually, we moved to my mom's. There were more things for the kids to do than at an apartment.

One weekend, my wife and I went to the ocean to camp by ourselves for the weekend. We ran into my younger brother and some of his friends. During conversation, one of his friends asked if there was a hell or were we living in it now? I told him there was a hell and it was certainly worse than anything on earth. I told him it was a place of everlasting torment and I sure didn't want to go there. I got a chance to share with him about Jesus.

We were all low on gas for the trip home. My wife and I prayed and we later found out that four of my brother's friends prayed too. We all got home safe and sound with empty tanks. Praise God!

Karen and I soon moved into a two bedroom duplex. Things were still real up and down. I guess it surprised us because we didn't think we'd have problems like this when we were both Christians and our marriage was based on God. We were real quick to point out the faults of the other one and to tell them they weren't acting like a Christian. We even talked about a divorce.

During the summer of 1984, we went camping with the kids and even the kids noticed we were at each other a lot. After I took the kids home, we sat down and talked. We decided neither one of us were living as children of God. So, we prayed and waited on the Lord about our marriage and the kids. God turned it around! We still have disagreements, but nothing like we did before. We learned that when we let our sinful nature take control, we have all sorts of problems. When we let the Lord take control, He does it right.

We told the kids that we were sorry and asked for their forgiveness, which they gave. We would all take turns praying at meal time and we began to have Bible study together. We would hold hands before bed and all take turns praying in a circle. We went to church every Sunday and took the kids with us when we had them. It wasn't long before the kids really looked forward to spending the weekend with us. They loved praying and going to church and they didn't do that at their mom's home.

Chapter Four

Rebuilding

Our problems are always our fault...we are taking control instead of letting God have control. Satan uses division to take you away from the Lord. He loves to make family members fight, disagree, hate each other. Family is God's plan and anything that is God's plan, Satan wants to destroy. It's important that we know that and that we recognize when Satan is attempting to create division in our family. We made this situation a matter of prayer and God answered our prayers.

We began to go fishing, swimming, camping and to the park as a family. We played baseball, football and board games as a family. But, most importantly, we talked and prayed as a family. As a result, we began to love one another with the love of Jesus.

I particularly remember one 4th of July when we went camping at Silver Lake. We had to take two cars because of the seat belt law. I had my son and his friend in my car and they both got sick, one in my car and one at the door of the tent. Then my youngest son got sick inside the tent. It seemed everyone was getting tired and cranky so we decided to find another place to camp. It was cold and rainy and most of the camping sites were full. We found one spot that everyone liked but me. The main reason was that there was a tavern nearby. Even though I was unanimously out-voted, we moved on. After a lot of driving, we drove to Silver Lake. We pitched our eight-man tent in the rain and cold.

We used the headlights of the car and two flashlights to accomplish putting up the tent. We finished in record time and everyone just went to sleep. The next morning, we all apologized to each other and extended forgiveness.

I usually do the cooking when we go camping. This time, I ran into lots of problems. I burned the pancakes and dropped the hamburgers into the fire.

The two youngest kids were supposed to stay out of the water, but the draw of the water was just to strong and before long they were in the water clothes and all. But, instead of getting upset, we took pictures of them and laughed. We spent part of our camping trips praying and reading the Bible as a family.

We went fishing and ate our catch for dinner. It was our custom to put up a sign at our campsite that said "Jesus is the Way." This seemed to attract other Christians and we met some great friends.

We now look back on all of those activities as what God used to bond us all together as a family. He built our relationships with each other and with Him as we spent time together.

Before long, we moved from the two-bedroom duplex to a one-bedroom apartment near the freeway in Auburn. Because Boeing was so close, the traffic made it very difficult to get to work and back. We had only been there a month when some Christian friends found a two bedroom house they thought would be perfect for us. It had a living room, dining room, kitchen, bathroom, utility room, garage, partial basement and front and back yards. The utility room was large enough to convert to a bedroom. We had been praying for a three-bedroom house, maybe this was it.

The owner of the house had evicted the last tenants and the very day he put up a "For Rent" sign our friends saw it and called him and then us. The owner said he would hold the house until we saw it.

We talked to the owner, but didn't have any money to pay a deposit. However, our friends said they would loan us the money for the deposit. I was working, but we were living paycheck to paycheck and had no savings. But, the Lord always provided. So, before we even saw the house, we agreed to take it. We were almost sorry for that decision. The house was filthy. There was garbage everywhere, it smelled, and it needed painting. The owner waived our damage deposit and instead we painted the house ourselves. I took five pickup loads and two car loads of garbage out of that house. We cleaned it up and got the smell out, painted it inside and out, got new carpets, new baseboard heaters and mowed the lawn and tended it until it was nice and green. We have been so blessed by God with our house and with Christian friends who really care about us.

Right around this time, a friend gave me a little button that says, "I Love Jesus" and I wear it every day. I call it my witness button.

I appreciate and thank God for the friends he has given us. We need each other as Christians. We need their ministry to us and we need to minister to them through His Holy Spirit.

This became more apparent when my mother and younger sister passed away. My mother became ill with cancer. She only lived two or three months after she was diagnosed. God answered our prayers by not letting her linger in pain. God took her home to prepare the way for my sister.

My sister's body was giving out. She lived a wild life, but at the end she realized she needed to change and was really trying. Two weeks after my mother died, my sister passed away. She is no longer suffering.

My daughter's third child was born with health problems and almost didn't live. Later, she had to be returned to the hospital. Today she is growing like a weed.

My other daughter's little girl needed to have brain surgery. We prayed to God for her safe keeping. The doctor said it's a miracle that she doesn't need the surgery now.

My older sister's son was electrocuted repairing a microwave. He was in ICU for a week and we didn't know how much brain damage he had or if he would even live. Our prayers were answered, and today he is fully recovered.

Once I gave myself to God, He has answered a lot of prayers. Thanks be to God!

Chapter Five

An Update

L et me share with you what God has done and continues to do in my life. At the end of this book is my favorite part...scriptures. Read the scriptures at the end and let God speak to your heart. He is real and alive and He loves you. You don't have to do anything for Him to accept you...He accepts you just as you are if you ask Him to. He wants us to love and serve Him.

God saved me from committing suicide, drinking, sniffing glue, drugs, fighting, a bad temper, mood swings, laziness, irresponsibility, sexual immorality, gang activity, slovenliness, and all sorts of trouble. I would like to have avoided all of those things, but my choices didn't allow me to. But, God in His mercy, allowed my choices to bring me to a point of knowing Him and of learning. Living out the consequences of our sinful choices is the most difficult of educations, but God can redeem all things. I feel real sorrow for others that were in trouble. I now listen to others, and show respect for my mom. I don't party anymore, I don't break the law anymore and I learned that without Jesus, I'm nothing!

The old man was headed for hell, but my new man is going to be with my Lord and Savior. Jesus Christ has provided eternal life in heaven with Him. I want you to remember one thing, we do not choose Jesus; He chooses us. He wants everyone of us to believe Him with our heart, confess Him with our mouth, obey Him with our actions, and trust Him with everything else. The one thing God gave each of us was a free will; we can choose to serve Jesus or the devil and the things of the world. Whatever happens isn't God's fault or the devil's fault, it's our fault because we are the ones that ultimately make our own choices.

John 5:16 says, "Ye have not chosen me, but I have chosen you, and ordained you, that ye should go and bring forth fruits, and that your fruit should remain; that whatsoever ye shall ask of the Father in my name, He may give it you."

One of my favorites, John 5:39 says, "Search the scriptures; for in them ye think ye have eternal life; and they are they which testify of me."

Psalm 37:5 says, "Commit thy way unto the Lord; trust also in Him; and He shall bring it to pass."

I am now enjoying being involved in a ministry. I purposely didn't attach a name to it because it belongs to the Lord. I can do nothing without Him.

I know that eventually we are going to travel, but that will be in God's timing, not mine. I envision a community for Jesus, Praise the Lord! This would be a place where runaways could find safety and help. It would be a place where young and old, married or single, rich or poor could come and learn about Jesus. We want to provide food, a prayer room, a Christian gift shop, worship, singing and a place for water baptism. We want to operate 24 hours a day. The doors would always be open and the phone would always be answered to those in need. We want to lead the way to Jesus and pray with those that want prayer, whenever they need it.

I believe this vision is from the Lord and He will open the doors at the right time.

I am excited at what the Lord is doing in me right now, as well as in the lives of my wife, kids, relatives and friends. I meet new Christian friends every day.

I know the decision to follow Christ is a difficult one. I have heard all kinds of excuses for not becoming a Christian and hear new ones every day. It's easier to blame someone else for our problems instead of taking responsibility for getting our lives changed through God. Will everything be great and always happy if you become a Christian? No, because we live in a world where sin is present. But, we can always go to God for help, strength, joy, peace and anything else we need. Prayer and Bible reading is important for each Christian, let it become a routine for you. Find a church where you can sing, rejoice, pray, worship, praise the Lord, fellowship with others and learn. It's easy to go to church on Sunday and live in the world the other six days...not just literally, but a worldly attitude. A good church should teach the entire Word of God, Jesus as Savior, and no other truth but Him. God will lead you to the church He wants you to be a part of if you ask Him Let everything in your life be a matter of prayer. Be lead of the Lord when you tell someone about Jesus, look at their heart; not their sin. John 3:16-17 says, "For God so loved the world, that He gave His only begotten son, that whoever believeth in Him should not perish, but have everlasting life. For God sent not His Son into the world to condemn the world; but that the world through Him Might be saved."

Chapter Six

Scriptures

Rom 10:9-10
9   That if thou shalt confess with thy mouth the Lord
Jesus, and shalt believe in thine heart that God hath raised
him from the dead, thou shalt be saved.
10   For with the heart man believeth unto righteousness;
and with the mouth confession is made unto salvation.
(KJV)

Now if you have confessed your sins unto the Lord and have believed in your heart that God sent Jesus to die for your sins and then raised Him from the dead, you are saved. But if you haven't confessed your sins all you have to do is say the sinners prayer to the Lord and mean it. Pray this prayer out loud right now if you want to accept Jesus.

Dear Father, forgive me for my sins; I know I'm a sinner and I believe that Jesus died for my sins and I ask Jesus to come into my life and to be my Lord and Savior. Father, Thank You for hearing my prayer and for forgiving me of my sins. I thank you for coming into my life and taking control of it. I also thank you for being my Lord and Savior. In Jesus name I pray. Amen

Rom 5:8
But God commendeth his love toward us, in that, while we were yet sinners, Christ died for us.

Rom 6:23
23 For the wages of sin is death; but the gift of God is eternal life through Jesus Christ our Lord.

Acts 10:34
34 And opening his mouth, Peter said: "I most certainly understand {now} that God is not one to show partiality,

Mark 8:36
36 "For what does it profit a man to gain the whole world, and forfeit his soul?

Prov 27:1
1 Do not boast about tomorrow, for you do not know what a day may bring forth.

1 Pet 3:18
18 For Christ also died for sins once for all, {the} just for {the} unjust, in order that He might bring us to God, having been put to death in the flesh, but made alive in the spirit;

I Jn 1:9
9 If we confess our sins, He is faithful and righteous to forgive us our sins and to cleanse us from all unrighteousness.

Ps 37:5
5 Commit your way to the LORD, trust also in Him, and He will do it.

1 Pet 5:8
8   Be of sober {spirit,} be on the alert. Your adversary, the devil, prowls about like a roaring lion, seeking someone to devour.

Prov 18:21
21   Death and life are in the power of the tongue, and those who love it will eat its fruit.

Acts 5:41
41   So they went on their way from the presence of the Council, rejoicing that they had been considered worthy to suffer shame for {His} name.

1 Pet 2:2
2   like newborn babes, long for the pure milk of the word, that by it you may grow in respect to salvation,

Gal 5:16
16   But I say, walk by the Spirit, and you will not carry out the desire of the flesh.

Gal 5:25
25   If we live by the Spirit, let us also walk by the Spirit.

Phil 4:6
6   Be anxious for nothing, but in everything by prayer and supplication with thanksgiving let your requests be made known to God.

Heb 10:25
25   not forsaking our own assembling together, as is the habit of some, but encouraging {one another} and all the more, as you see the day drawing near.

John 8:31-32

31 Jesus therefore was saying to those Jews who had believed Him, "If you abide in My word, {then} you are truly disciples of Mine;

32 and you shall know the truth, and the truth shall make you free."

Col 1:13-14

13 For He delivered us from the domain of darkness, and transferred us to the kingdom of His beloved Son,

14 in whom we have redemption, the forgiveness of sins.

Luke 10:19-20

19 "Behold, I have given you authority to tread upon serpents and scorpions, and over all the power of the enemy, and nothing shall injure you.

20 "Nevertheless do not rejoice in this, that the spirits are subject to you, but rejoice that your names are recorded in heaven."

Ram 8:37

37 But in all these things we overwhelmingly conquer through Him who loved us.

1 Jn 4:4

4 You are from God, little children, and have overcome them; because greater is He who is in you than he who is in the world.

2 Cor 5:17

17 Therefore if any man is in Christ, {he is} a new creature; the old things passed away; behold, new things have come.

Col 2:14-15
14   having canceled out the certificate of debt consisting of decrees against us {and} which was hostile to us; and He has taken it out of the way, having nailed it to the cross.
15   When He had disarmed the rulers and authorities, He made a public display of them, having triumphed over them through Him.

2 Cor 4:16
16   Therefore we do not lose heart, but though our outer man is decaying, yet our inner man is being renewed day by day.

2 Cor 4:18
18   while we look not at the things which are seen, but at the things which are not seen; for the things which are seen are temporal, but the things which are not seen are eternal.

Matt 6:33
33   "But seek first His kingdom and His righteousness; and all these things shall be added to you.

Matt 6:19-21
19   "Do not lay up for yourselves treasures upon earth, where moth and rust destroy, and where thieves break in and steal.
20   "But lay up for yourselves treasures in heaven, where neither moth nor rust destroys, and where thieves do not break in or steal;
21   for where your treasure is, there will your heart be also.

Ps 1:2-3
2   But his delight is in the law of the LORD, and in His law he meditates day and night.

3   And he will be like a tree {firmly} planted by streams of water, which yields its fruit in its season, and its leaf does not wither; and in whatever he does, he prospers.

Phil 4:6-7

6   Be anxious for nothing, but in everything by prayer and supplication with thanksgiving let your requests be made known to God.

7   And the peace of God, which surpasses all comprehension, shall guard your hearts and your minds in Christ Jesus.

Mark 7:6-8

6   And He said to them, "Rightly did Isaiah prophesy of you hypocrites, as it is written, 'This people honors Me with their lips, but their heart is far away from me.

7   'But in vain do they worship me, teaching as doctrines the precepts of men.

8   "Neglecting the commandment of God, you hold to the tradition of men."

Eph 4:14-15

14   As a result, we are no longer to be children, tossed here and there by waves, and carried about by every wind of doctrine, by the trickery of men, by craftiness in deceitful scheming;

15   but speaking the truth in love, we are to grow up in all {aspects} into Him, who is the head, {even} Christ,

Eph 4:29

29   Let no unwholesome word proceed from your mouth, but only such {a word} as is good for edification according to the need {of the moment,} that it may give grace to those who hear.

Titus 2:1

1   But as for you, speak the things which are fitting for sound doctrine.

Heb 13:8-9

8   Jesus Christ {is} the same yesterday and today, {yes} and forever.

9   Do not be carried away by varied and strange teachings; for it is good for the heart to be strengthened by grace, not by foods, through which those who were thus occupied were not benefited.

James 4:7

7   Submit therefore to God. Resist the devil and he will flee from you.

Col 2:20-23

20   If you have died with Christ to the elementary principles of the world, why, as if you were living in the world, do you submit yourself to decrees, such as,

21   "Do not handle, do not taste, do not touch!"

22   (which all {refer to} things destined to perish with the using)- in accordance with the commandments and teachings of men?

23   These are matters which have, to be sure, the appearance of wisdom in self-made religion and self-abasement and severe treatment of the body, {but are} of no value against fleshly indulgence.

Rev 12:11

11   "And they overcame him because of the blood of the Lamb and because of the word of their testimony, and they did not love their life even to death.

James 3:17

17   But the wisdom from above is first pure, then peace-able, gentle, reasonable, full of mercy and good fruits, unwavering, without hypocrisy.
(NAS)

John 10:10) The thief cometh not, (the devil) but for to steal, and to kill, and to destroy: I am come (JESUS CHRIST) that they might have life, and that they have it more abundantly.

The devil uses many forms of stress to destroy us; Here are some of them:

1.) Death of a spouse, child, friend, relative, or someone closes to you.
2.) A divorce
3.) A separation from your mate
4.) Major personal injury or illness
5.) Jail or some other institution
6.) Marriage at any age
7.) Losing or retiring from your job
8.) Your health
9.) Behavior patterns
10.) Sexual difficulties
11.) Someone new in your family
12.) Your finances or your business
13.) Different line of work
14.) Anger and argument with others
15.) Making a loan for a house, car, boat, material things, credit cards, bills, etc.
16.) In-law problems
17.) When you had two incomes and now you have one
18.) Your living conditions
19.) Change in your residence, school, church, vaca-tion, etc.

20.) Eating habits
21.) The holidays
22.) Losing sleep
23.) Medications
24.) Physical condition, over weight
25.) Smoking, drinking, liquor, drugs, etc.
26.) To much caffeine and sugar
27.) Abuse = physical, verbally, violence, oral or sexual molestation, assaulted, or some other abuse
28.) Being handicapped
29.) Being a foster child
30.) Losing a pet
31.) Peer pressure, trying to meet others expectation or standards
32.) I'm sure you can add more to this list.

As you can see the devil wants to destroy you and he doesn't want you to Know anything about GOD!

Let me ask you some other things that the devil likes to do in your life.

Do you feel angry, hate, sad, shyness, embarrassment, inferior to others, do you feel like a mistake, unworthy, I don't care attitude, self centered or selfless, unloved, defensive, humiliation, blame others, guilt, an outsider, loneliness, mind reading, pain, fear, sadness, I'm bad, I'll never be any good, its my fault, unhappy, or? As you can see that there's a lot to deal with in our lives and in this world. How we deal with it is up to each and everyone of us. With GODS help we can make it and GOD can lead us to the right person to help us; a pastor, another Christian, a spiritual counselor, a professional in the area you seeking help for. We ALL deal with emotions. We have to take our emotions one day at a time. Lets look at the three top emotions = anger, fear, and discouragement. Anger can be used constructively or destructfully.

If we don't deal with it correctly someone is going to get hurt. We don't have to be a victim of our circumstances!!! We don't need to fear; Fear is not from GOD, its from the devil and he uses fear in many forms of our everyday life. You can overcome fear with GOD. The devil also uses discouragement in many ways and forms. GOD can lift you up! The devil tears you down. Which one will you choose? GOD or the devil?

As I sit here writing, thinking, and praying on what to write; I feel like GOD is telling me to be myself and used myself as a example. I've been through a lot of things in my own life. I'm 58 years old as I write this book.

There are many forms of emotions and stress. There is a GOD, JESUS CHRIST, HOLY-SPIRIT, AND ANGELS.

There is also a devil, demons, evil forces, and evil men. I know my old man did evil things. I was saved in 1979. GOD came into my life, saved me and forgave me of my sins. I have a new man and I like my new man and I don't want anything to do with my old man and his ways anymore. GOD has been ministering to me and by the HOLY-SPIRIT guiding, leading, directing my paths. The BIBLE is my sword and a lamp unto my feet, it has everything in it pertaining to this life, it has everything in it to help me through things that I face in life. My hope and prayer is that you will know GOD and change your life around before its too late.

2 Corinthians 4: 3-4) 3 – But if our gospel be hid, it is hid to them that are lost: 4 – whom the god of this world (the devil) hath blinded the minds of them which believe not, lest the light of the glorious gospel of CHRIST, who is the image of GOD, should shine unto them.

I was there once; Thank GOD I'm not anymore GLORY TO GOD!

Isaiah 55:6) Seek ye the LORD while HE may be found, call ye upon HIM while HE is near:

We don't know what a day is going to bring. We don't know when we are going to die. We don't know when JESUS is going to return.

You need to be born again (SAVED) before you die or before JESUS returns cause after you die or JESUS returns its all over with, there's not another chance!

You have a choice to make! Where are you going to spend eternity? With the devil or with GOD? I hope and pray that you choose GOD!!!

Chapter Seven

The lost unsaved

2 Corinthians 5:17) Therefore if any man be in CHRIST, he is a new creature: old things are passed away; behold, all things are become new.

Everyone is going through something. What are you going through?

I'm going to use some of the things that I went through in my life. Maybe you can relate to some of them. My earthly dad was an alcoholic, all he cared about was liquor and cigarettes. Thank GOD he was saved, at least that's what I was told by a group of Christians standing in a circle holding hands and praying with him. He was abusive. We were taken away by the authorities and put in foster homes for 2 years. I remember growing up we didn't have much, we had two shirts, a pair of pants and a pair of shoes. We moved from town to town, school to school, had to make new friends ALL the time. it was about 5 years old when I was molested by a family member. Junior High school I started smoking, drinking, drugs, had a bad attitude, temper, anger, lying, stealing, not listening, sniffing glue, fighting, ran around with the rough bunch, I wanted to fit in, I wanted to be somebody; any way you get the general idea.

I was 28 years old when JESUS came into my life and saved me. I changed step by step, day by day with GODS help. It wasn't ALL at once and it was not easy at first.

Don't give up, hang in there, things will get better. You can change your life around. You can put on the new man and take off the old man and his ways. Maybe you think that you're a mistake, inferior to others, fear intimacy, feel selfless, worthless, unloved, blame someone else, guilt, its my fault, I'm an outsider, loneliness, ashamed, or? There are many, many feelings that we can add to this list.

Don't listen to the devil and his lies!

GOD made you and HE cares for YOU, Loves YOU and HE wants to save YOU.

Survivors of sexual abuse often block out feelings. I know I did. We hid it and lock it away, if we don't get help support and treatment when we are younger or in our youth, an adult we can experience all sort of post traumatic stress disorder, that can include nightmares, panic attacks and memories and into our relationships. Most of the time it is a family member that is doing the sexual abusing. Without help we can be robbed of feeling emotionally and sexually safe and secure. It doesn't matter what it is that were going through, if we don't get help, support, and treatment; the devil is going to cause all kinds of emotions and feelings. Emotions can be used constructively or they can be used destruct fully. Don't try to solve all of your problems at once. Remember one thing if you are seeking help, be honest and truthful, be honest and truthful with GOD.

Proverbs 12:22) Lying lips are abomination to the LORD: but they that deal truly are HIS delight.

Lets talk about marriage:

Marriage is to be between a man and a women.

Deuteronomy 24:1) When a man hath taken a wife, and married her, and it come to pass that she find no favour in his eyes, because he hath found some uncleanness in her: then let him write her a bill of divorcement, and give it in her hand, and send her out of his house.

GOD does not want you to get a divorce just because you feel like getting one, it has to be for some kind of uncleanness. This can be for husbands or wives. It can be for abuse, unfaithfulness, an affair, drunkard, drug addict, verbally abusive, adultery, bodily harm. These are just some of the reasons.

GOD wants both of you to be saved! You have to work your problems out, pray together, talk, communicate. It can't be ALL one sided. Its a lot easier when you both are saved. (Christians) I'm not saying that Christian marriages don't have problems cause they do. Together with GODS help you can work them out. You have to be willing to work things out. Day after day we have to make decisions, choices that affect both of us. Now if your divorce and remarried you have a set of new problems to work out. You both come from different back grounds, have different point of views, different expectations, you both might have children and you have to consider there feelings also. I'm remarried and my kids didn't accept my wife right away. It wasn't very easy. They were very verbally abusive to her, didn't listen to her, called her names, tried to break us up. My wife and I talked and we prayed to GOD for help. We have been married for 24 years now as I'm writing this book.

You also have inlaw problems, relatives, friends, co workers, everyone wants to give you advice but you have to sort it all out. Some of it is good and some of it is bad. No one else can live your life or make your decisions for you. The decisions you make will decide how your going to live your life.

There are three things about the future:

1.) It is not going to be like the past.
2.) It is not going to be exactly the way we think its going to be.
3.) The rate of change will take place faster than we can imagine.

You can poke fun at me, mock me, call me names or whatever, that's your choice. I will be praying for you. I want to win souls for the kingdom of GOD while there's still time. Amen

Here's a sinners prayer – Father in heaven I come to you in JESUS name. I'm a sinner forgive me of my sins, wash me in the blood of JESUS. Father GOD help me to put on the new man and change my life. Father GOD guide, lead, direct my paths. LORD help me to make the right decisions. Father GOD thank you for hearing my prayer. LORD thank you for forgiving me of my sins. LORD thank you for washing me in your blood. LORD thank you for my new man. LORD thank you for saving my life. LORD thank you for guiding, leading, and directing my paths. LORD thank you for helping me make the right decisions in JESUS name. AMEN.

Tell someone you are saved. Find a church to belong to for the fellowship, teaching, for prayer; one that believes and teaches about GOD, JESUS, HOLY SPIRIT AND THE HOLY BIBLE as the true WORD of GOD. You need the fellowship, teaching and prayer.

Chapter Eight

Backsliders

Jeremiah 3:22) Return, ye backsliding children, and I will heal your backslidings. Behold, we come unto thee; for thou art the LORD OUR GOD.

Backsliders

I want to talk to you backsliders. Why did you backslide? Could it be a lack of FAITH? Lack of wisdom? Lack of understanding, pride, leaning on your own understanding? You blame someone else for your backsliding? Weakness, haven't given up your old ways and habits? You want to fit in with others? What's the reason? The first year that I was saved I backslid I wanted to fit in with others. I thought I was somebody when I wasn't and so on. I went to a tavern and I heard this voice saying Ray, Ray what are you doing? You've been saved. After that night I went home and got on my knees and cried out to the LORD to forgive me. That's when I really started changing.

You might say __ you don't know what I've done, the LORD won't forgive me, I can't come back to the LORD.

Yes you can, don't let the devil keep you in chains, in bondage. Don't listen to the lies of the devil.

JESUS will forgive you for your backsliding's. All you have to do is ask JESUS to forgive you and turn from your wicked ways. Then you have to make things right. You have to pay for what you did. JESUS will be with you. Remember this one thing Where are you going to spend eternity? In heaven with GOD or in hell with the devil. Its about JESUS and your eternal salvation. Here's some scriptures of what could happen:

1 Timothy 4:1-2) 1 Now the spirit speaketh expressly, that in the latter times some shall depart from the faith, giving heed to seducing spirits, and doctrines of devils:

2 Speaking lies in hypocrisy; having their conscience seared with a hot

iron;

2Timothy 4: 3-4) 3— For the time will come when they will not endure sound doctrine; but after their own lusts shall they heap to themselves teachers, having itching ears: 4 And they shall turn away their ears from the truth, and shall be turned unto fables.

Proverbs 16:18) Pride goeth before destruction, and an haughty spirit before the fall.

Do you fall into one of these categories?

1 Corinthians 1:17) For CHRIST sent me not to baptize, but to preach the gospel: not with wisdom of words, lest the cross of CHRIST should be made of none effect:

18. For the preaching of the cross is to them that perish foolishness; but unto us which are saved it is the power of GOD.

11 Corinthians 2: 4-5) 4 And my speech and my preaching was not with enticing words of mans wisdom, but in demonstration of the SPIRIT and of power.

5   That your faith should not stand in the wisdom of men, but in the power of GOD. I have to let you know that you can be forgiven for your backslidings, no matter what it is. Say this prayer – Father GOD forgive me; say it whatever it is. Father GOD I want to be a child of GOD. Father GOD I want to go to heaven.

Father GOD thank you for forgiving me of my backslidings. Father GOD thank you for making me your child again. Father GOD thank you for receiving me into heaven; in JESUS name Amen. Hang in there, I'll be praying for you.

Chapter Nine

Men's Traditions

Mark 7: 8-9) 8 – For laying aside the commandment of GOD, ye hold the tradition of men, as the washing of pots and cups: and many other such like things ye do. 9 – and he said unto them, full well ye reject the commandment of GOD, that ye may keep your own tradition.

Your kinda like the backsliders.

You're following men traditions.

Your letting men deceive you with there enticing words, where they lay in wait to deceive you. Man plays on your weakness, your lack of understanding.

Read – Revelation 2: 4-5) 4 Nevertheless I have some-what against thee, because thou hast left thy first love. 5 – Remember therefore from whence thou art fallen, and repent, and do the first works; or else I will come unto thee quickly, and will remove thy candlestick out of his place, except thou repent.

Remember every man has to answer to GOD. My prayer is for you not to fellow men's traditions and for you to get out of man's ways and get closer to GOD; to know JESUS CHRIST on a personal level!

Say this prayer Father GOD forgive me for following man's traditions. Father GOD bring me out of (whatever your in) and bring me closer to YOU so I can have a personal relationship with YOU! Father GOD thank you for forgiving me for following man's traditions. Father GOD thank you for bringing me out of (whatever it is) and for giving me a personal relationship with YOU. In JESUS CHRIST name Amen.

I'll be praying for you. GOD-BLESS

Mark 11:4) Therefore I say unto you, what things so ever ye desire, when ye pray, believe that ye receive them, and ye shall have them.

Chapters Ten

Christians

GOD has put Christians on my heart. We struggle with a lot of things and some things needlessly. One of the biggest reasons that we struggle is we don't use our time wisely. We are always in a hurry; have our own plans and we think that we don't have enough time to do what GOD wants us to do. We say I can't do that, I don't know how, I am not good at that, I didn't go to school for that, I'm not a Pastor or we think that we don't need to go to church to believe in GOD, I can stay at home; Yes, and that's what the devil wants you to do; cause when he has you alone he can work on you easier and put all kinds of thoughts in your head; he can get us to dwell on the past, we think about tomorrow or even way ahead of time. We go to church every Sunday because it's our duty as a Christian. We think it's all up to the Pastor's for people's salvation. We criticize Pastor's, the church, members of the church, denominations; this is not what GOD wants us to do. We come up with all kinds of excuses and blame someone else, we leave the church and find another one; some of us are church hoppers. We can't grow and learn anything about GOD or grow closer to

GOD when we act in those ways. We also say I don't know how to pray, my prayers are not very good. The list goes on, I'm sure you can add some. Reads – Acts 10:34) Then Peter opened his month, and said, of a truth I perceive that GOD is no respecter of persons:

GOD is no respecter of persons, what He has done for others, HE will also do it for you.

Mark 8:36) For what shall it profit a man, if he shall gain the whole world, and lose his own soul?

You can gain the whole world, money, fame, prosperity, friends, material things and the list goes on. What about your soul? Think about it!

Proverbs 27:1) Boast not thyself of tomorrow; for thou knowest not what a day may bring forth.

Matthew 6:34) Take therefore no thought for the in morrow: Or the morrow shall take thought for the things of itself. Sufficient unto the day is the evil thereof.

Why do we try and cram so much into a day? This is one way that we get stressed out; we have all kinds of emotions and say I can't take it anymore. We try to cram our today's into tomorrow's we need to take it one day at a time.

Proverbs 18:21) Death and life are in the power of the tongue: and they that love it shall eat the fruit thereof.

Psalm 133:1) Behold, how good and how pleasant it is for brethren to dwell together in UNITY!

Chapter Eleven

Denominations

R omans 3:10) As it is written, there is none righteous, no, not one:

Romans 3:23) For all have sinned, and come short of the glory of GOD:

Revelation 7:9) After this I beheld, and, 1, a great multitude, which no man could number, of all nations, and kindreds, and people, and tongues, stood before the throne, and before the LAMB, clothed with white robes, and palms in their hands:

I'm writing this to ALL DENOMINATIONS! Brethren we must stop devouring one another, falsely accusing each other, backbiting, whispering, gossiping, and such. We need to let others know who JESUS is and about their ETERNAL SALVATION; Where are they going to spend ETERNITY?

We also build up walls with our denominations, judge each other, and say things about each other; Brothers and Sisters this should not be!!! How can WE shine for JESUS? What kind of a example are WE showing?

We need to come together in the name of JESUS CHRIST! We need to PRAY for each other! Yes, WE need to protect ourselves who WE fellowship with. Remember this;

Whoever is with us, for us, Whoever believes in the name of JESUS CHRIST is with us, not against us. The devil has us just where he wants us; Building walls up, against each other, and divided against each other and so on.

Can you imagine what WE could do for GOD if WE join our forces together in the name of JESUS CHRIST? Lets keep the devil on the run!

We go to our churches, have our programs, events, and so on during the week, we do it week after week there's nothing wrong with that, we need to.

I'm asking for us to pray for each other and to UNITE together against the forces of evil in the name of JESUS CHRIST:

GOD gave HIS SON who HE loved to save us.

JESUS CHRIST took our sins upon HIMSELF so that we can be forgiven and saved.

JESUS was buried and rose the third day conquering death for us JESUS went to heaven and sent the comforter to us, which is the HOLY-SPIRIT, which lives in our hearts; to guide, lead, and to direct our paths; to teach us and so on. The BIBLE is a lamp unto our feet, it has the answers to life and the do's and dont's examples for us and so on.

Its not about your background, race, color, nationality, or? JESUS said that we ALL have sinned.

Chapter Twelve

I hope and pray that YOU accept this free gift from GOD of eternal life. There's only one way to be saved and that's through JESUS CHRIST the SON of GOD!!! Here is a card that I got for my birthday one year.

Here are some pictures on a missions trip to Mexico: Mud hut with me leaning against it with eggs, by the way my nick name is eggman because of it; the shower, outhouse, some of the kids in Mexico.

Christian Brothers and Sisters in India: A loving family of CHRIST with a ministry. Their new church, youth group, the children, Sunday school.

Sum Kim his Pastor and myself, sum Kim's wife, and other Korean's being baptized.

Walt my christian brother who is black and went to his heavenly home.

Co-workers myself, Ukrainian and from Poland, myself and Philippine brother.

As you can see; GOD is for everyone, not a certain group of people.

Happy Birthday, Ray!

This card reminds me of you….. because you always show so much love for all of God's children – red, yellow, black & white, young & old. You are a great blessing to all who know you.

Have a good year!
Love, Ruth & Bryan ???

Mission Trip Mexico
Community Out house

Children Mexico
Mission Trip

Mission Trip Mexico
Mud Hut

India Ministry Team

Church in India

Children's Sunday School, India

Youth India

Children's Sunday School, India

Sum Kim - His Pastor, Myself

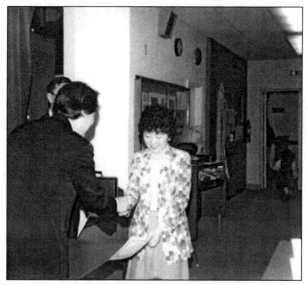

Sum Kim's Wife Baptized

Sum Kim
Church Congregation

Brother Walt & Myself

Myself
Polish Ukraine Brothers

Phillipino Brother

My best friend Wayne knows my old man
and my new man.

I said the sinners prayer with him.
Glory to God

Revelation 12:11) And they overcame him (the devil) by the blood of the LAMB, and by the WORD of their testimony, and they loved not their lives unto the death.

Chapter Thirteen

Praise reports and prayer request

Here are some praise reports and prayer requests that people have sent me, over the internet, a co-worker, one from a family member, and friend.

Kent, Washington – To the very best friend who's always there; to listen to my problems it really means a lot to me. Thank you

My son I know that I'm different looking than your other friends, like my hair, earrings and tattoo's. I look this way because it's what I like, I enjoy looking this way I'm thankful for all that you have done for me. I know I can't take back what I've done but I hope 1 can be forgiven, thank you for forgiving me.

Milton, Washington – I've been remiss in not sending my thanks sooner for the lovely plant for Secretary week, forgive me.

Federal Way Washington – This is the Jim first time in my life anyone outside of my family has honored me. What a joy to he so blest. May God bless you real good.

Singapore – I wanna thank GOD for HIS awesome change in me. I've been going through lots of stuff, emotionally and physically as well. I tried doing: things with my own strength, but I found out that I can only do all things through CHRIST who strengthens me! It was a long lesson to learn but I give GOD all the glory, honour and praise because, HE's molding me and changing me from glory to Amen!

USA – I was saved 17 years ago, but I soon forgot the ways a Christian should live I thought just getting saved was all I needed. I know GOD can take other cravings from me, and I also got into a local church and began studying HIS WORD I found that the more I learn about GOD, the more I want to learn! Trust in JESUS, for HE has an ultimate plan for you and I.

U.S.A. – Eleven years ago we were losing our home, our marriage and our children were so sad that no one would ever see them smile. We needed JESUS in our life but did not know how until we went to church after a dear sister kept on asking us to go. My husband sat on one side and I on the other, We were both so mad. GOD showed me that night HIS power and just how much HE loved us. We received JESUS that night. Delivered from drugs and alcohol and today we walk with HIM daily. We love each other more and more than the day we got married, Without GOD in our marriage we truly would not be here today. We give HIM all the honour and glory. PRAISE THE LORD.

Tokyo Japan – When I feel lost, I'll pray to JESUS CHRIST for direction. I feel that JESUS CHRIST is always beside me and I say my prayers every night.

Philippines – I PRAISE GOD for all the good things HE has done in my life. HIS love is great, it covers the wide expanse of heaven and earth.

U.S.A. – I would like to tell everyone that GOD is still in the job of deliverance. I have been delivered from drugs and alcohol for 8 years now.

I wrote this to tell others that GOD can and will break your desire for those things that seem unbearable and unstoppable. HE can and HE will. PRAISE GOD.

U.S.A. – So for the last twelve years, I've been going to the prisons in Florida with the message and also have penpals, I relate the message too. I also have inmates on death row, GOD has blessed me with. I'm blessed that what the devil meant for evil, GOD turned it around for good.

U.S.A. – Well, here I am, 58 years old and for the first time in my life I feel contented, at peace, and happy. The LORD can bring you out of bondage too. It is only when we give up our life to CHRIST control that we are truly set free. To save your life, you must first give it back to HIM who created it. You are never too old to give your life to GOD, but, you can be too late! May the love and sacrifice of our LORD and SAVIOR, CHRIST JESUS, give you peace.

Zambia – Imagine the joy JESUS feels when someone receives salvation through HIS testimony shared by one Christian to an unsaved soul! Never give up on people around you.

Australia –I challenge all of you who read this, that no matter how old you are – 13 like me or 98, start praying and ask JESUS into your life.

U.S.A. – The LORD means a lot to me. He has helped me in so many ways. Through life's ups and downs HE was here, man was HE there. The LORD has always been there, even when the devil would say just throw your hands up and end it all. The LORD would say no I am here for you, you can make it. Through everything, the LORD has given me strength in many ways, through my mistakes along the way HE has been there even in the most weakest points.

I thank the LORD, thank you JESUS.

U.S.A. – All my life I'd been the center of ridicule, rejection, and abuse; but, as its been told, all things are done for a purpose. I hated my life, I hated everything about who I was. I prayed so many times that GOD would take my life. I was rejected and unloved. I grew up in poverty, oppression, violence, and death. There were times I attempted to commit suicide, I wanted so much to leave this world, I just wanted to forget it all and be free. I was arrested by the police and sentenced to serve the remainder of my life in prison. I sat down and asked GOD to come into my life and accept me into HIS home. I started to go through a transformation spiritually. I joined the prison church's and became active in every program that was offered. I learned the truth of GOD and the LORD JESUS CHRIST. As GOD opens my eyes and heart, I give thanks to HIM each and every day that I wake up and see this world. I was once blind and bitter, but now I am what GOD wishes for me to be, HIS child.

U.S.A. – I had been going to see all kinds of shrinks and therapists and clinic type people ever since I was a toddler. I had been diagnosed with p d d (Pervasive Developmental Disorder) age 13, I was diagnosed with schizophrenia. 9th grade I was put in a segregated class with all the dysfunctional/criminal kids. I spiraled downwards. I was on the boarder line of legal insanity. The medication made me a zombie, Then I was at a youth retreat for teen challenge, Orange County. They prayed over me near the end of the service; and I was healed. I was healed indeed. The symptoms never came back. I thank the LORD 100% first and foremost, and I thank all the people that believed in me no matter what the professionals thought.

Philippines – There are times I stumble and fall but HIS grace is sufficient for me. I may struggle from trails and even with my own weaknesses, but HIS presence never abandons me. GOD is good all the time.

U.S.A. – In the church that I go to, you feel the HOLY-SPIRIT there. I am hungry for GOD I have a relationship with HIM not religion.

England – I thank GOD that I will soon reach the age of 67 because I didn't really get to know HIM until I turned 50. I had been in and out of churches and chapels since I was 14 years old. Some of those chapels I attended while in prison doing time. However I can say that through all those years GOD had HIS hand upon me.

U.S.A. – Without JESUS, I am sure I would be very unhappy, honestly don't know if I would even be here. Before HE was in my life, I carried a tremendous amount of burden on my shoulders, I worried about so many things that it was eating me up inside. Loss of family members, illness, job difficulties, finances. The problems we all face. Since HE has entered my life, I have placed everything in HIS hands. I'm not saying the life of a Christian is perfect, we still face troubles, but HE is there to guide our steps and opens a new door when one is closed. The words in the scriptures are always a comfort to me. I feel when

I read them daily I am stronger. They are GODS instructions to us and are as important as food to our bodies, If someone is reading this and wondering whether to let JESUS into their life, all I can say is if you want peace, joy, contentment, and eternal life, let HIM in, ask HIM into your life. HE is waiting for your invitation.

India – PRAISE GOD some accepted JESUS CHRIST through your powerful testimony book. We distributed all the books in so many places and we got tremendous response. PRAISE GOD. We want to reprint your book in our language. Because at this moment we are travelling 50 many places more than before. We believe your witness will shake more people if we have more copies of it.

Prayer Request's

Bangladesh – We are leaving for a 10 day trip to our new converts area. We will visit North Bengal, Mymenshing,

Koligrain and Jassore. Please pray for our save journey and divine protection. Please also pray for our needy brethren whose houses have fallen down by heavy rain. Pray for my younger daughter.

Iran – Pray for my Father and grand Moms salvation. GOD works in their church and country.

India – Pray for my career, marriage and ministry. I'm experiencing a lot of satanic hindrance and obstacles in each matter, I ask for your sincere and fervent prayers.

U.S.A. – Pray for my son 7 years old who has cancer. He is currently receiving chemo and radiation. Please pray for his complete healing. Thank you!

China – One of my colleagues father is suffering from stomach cancer and for his salvation.

U.S.A. – Pray for my company it is near bankruptcy and I am about to lose my job.

U.S.A. – Husband needs salvation and for their marriage.

U.S.A. – My friends daughter is doing drugs and has run away, please pray for them.

U.S.A. – Pray for my wife to come back home and restore our marriage.

Single mother with three Sons; divorce and father is in and out of their lives. Lost her job. Pray for the children ages 8, 12, and 15.

U.S.A. – My daughter is 22 and a heroin addict. She almost died 4 times because of it. She is in her 6th rehab center. Pray for her salvation and her deliverance.

U.S.A. – Pray for my husband and our marriage; and me, Thank you

China – Pray that I teach correctly and absolutely according to the Bible.

I really thank you for caring for me and praying for me!

These next prayer request are from children in India. Pray for my studies and my family and my father who is central prison.

Pray for my education and my family.

Pray for my father, mother and sister.

Pray for my salvation and education.

Pray for my salvation and for my family's needs.

Pray for my family and a new car.

Pray for my studies and family.

Pray for my education and family. I want to be used by GOD among children.

Pray for my education and family. I repented and accepted JESUS CHRIST as my personal Savior. Please pray for me and for my Sunday School and friends.

Pray for my studies and salvation. Pray for my father; Pray for all of us.

Pray for my family, especially my father. I want to grow in my spiritual life.

Please pray for me and my legs, I'm not able to walk. Pray for my brother who is carrying me everywhere.

Pray for my health, studies and family.

Chapter Fourteen

Praise reports and prayer request

W hatever comes out of your mouth is the fruit your going to eat. If its evil, you will eat evil fruit and if its good, you will eat good fruit. What you speak is what you get, it comes right back to you. Who ever said, sticks and stones will break my bones but words will never hurt me That is a lie, cause words do HURT! Words can build a person up or tear a person down. Think before you speak.

Ephesians (4:14-15) 14 That we henceforth be no more children, tossed to and fro, and carried about with every wind of doctrine, by the sleight of men, and cunning craftiness, whereby they lie in wait to deceive; 15 But speaking the truth in love, may grow up into him in all things, which is the head, even CHRIST:

Why are we listening to man? Instead of GOD!

Why are we following man? Instead of GOD!

Why are we believing man? Instead of GOD!

Could it be that we want to hear what we want to hear? We are ALL looking for something!

Matthew (24:3-4) 3 And as HE sat upon the mount of olives, the disciples came unto HIM privately, saying, tell us, when shall these things be? And what shall be the sign of thy coming, and of the end of the world? 4 And JESUS answered and said unto them, take heed that no man deceive you.

Read the whole chapter. Why then are some of us being deceived by man? The world is not going to end, it's going to end as we know it. Man is going to destroy it by nuclear war: Man wants to wipe Israel off the face of the earth.

Here are three scriptures for you.

1.) John (10:10) The thief cometh not, (the devil) but for to steal, and to kill, and to destroy: I am (JESUS CHRIST) come that they might have life, and that they might have it more abundantly. (remind the devil what JESUS promised YOU!)

2.) James (4:7) Submit yourselves therefore to GOD. Resist the devil, and he will flee from you.
(Let the devil know that you're a child of the living GOD and what JESUS CHRIST has done for YOU.)

3.) Mark (11:22-26) 23 – For verily I say unto you, that whosoever shall say unto this mountain, Be thou removed, and be thou cast into the sea: and shall not doubt in his heart, but shall believe that those things which he saith shall come to pass; he shall have whatsoever he saith.

4.) 24 – Therefore I say unto you, what things so ever ye desire, when ye pray, believe that ye receive them, and ye shall have them.

Whatever YOUR facing in life, that is YOUR mountain, YOU need to believe in YOUR heart.

YOU received the answer to YOUR prayer and it has been removed and cast out of YOUR life.

Some are easier than others. YOU have to grow in YOUR faith and grow closer to GOD. The more YOU do, the easier it becomes!

I have 39 things that you can remind yourself of who you are and remind the devil also.

Say these I am's –

I am...

1. **A Child of God** *(Romans 8:16)*
2. **Redeemed from the hand of the enemy** *(Psalms 107:2)*
3. **Forgiven** *(Colossians 1:13, 14)*
4. **Saved by Grace through Faith** *(Ephesians 2:8)*
5. **Justified** *(Romans 5:1)*
6. **Sanctified** *(I Corinthians 6:11)*
7. **A New Creature** *(II Corinthians 5:17)*
8. **Partaker of His Divine Nature** *(II Peter 1:?)*
9. **Redeemed from the Curse of the Law** *(Galatians 3:13)*
10. **Delivered from the powers of darkness** *(Colossians 1:13)*
11. **Led by the Spirit of God** *(Romans 8:14)*
12. **A Son of God** *(Romans 8:14)*
13. **Kept in safety wherever I go** *(Psalms 91:11)*
14. **Getting all my needs met by Jesus** *(Philippians 4:19)*
15. **Casting all my cares on Jesus** *(I Peter 5:7)*
16. **Strong in the Lord and in the Power of His Might** *(Ephesians 6:10)*
17. **Doing all things through Christ who strengthens me** *(Philippines 4:13)*
18. **An heir of God and a joint heir with Jesus** *(Romans 8:17)*
19. **Heir to the blessings of Abraham** *(Galatians 3:13, 14)*
20. **Observing and doing the Lord's commandments** *(Deuteronomy 28:12)*
21. **Blessed coming in and going out** *(Deuteronomy 28:6)*
22. **An inheritor of eternal life** *(I John 5:11 & 12)*
23. **Blessed with all spiritual blessing** *(Ephesians 1:3)*
24. **HEALED BY HIS STRIPES** *(I Peter 2:24)*
25. **Exercising my authority over the enemy** *(Luke 10:19)*
26. **Above only and not beneath** *(Deuteronomy 28:13)*
27. **More than a conqueror** *(Romans 8:37)*
28. **Establishing God's Word here on earth** *(Matthew 16:19)*
29. **An overcomer by the Blood of the Lamb and Word of my Testimony** *(Rev. 12:11)*
30. **Daily overcoming the devil** *(I John 4:4)*
31. **Not moved by what I see** *(II Corinthians 4:18)*
32. **Walking by faith and not by sight** *(II Corinthians 5:7)*
33. **Casting down vain imaginations** *(II Corinthians 10:4 & 5)*
34. **Bringing every thought into captivity** *(II Corinthians 10:5)*
35. **Being transformed by a renewed mind** (Romans 12:1 & 2)
36. **A laborer together with God** *(I Corinthians 3:9)*
37. **The righteousness of God in Christ** *(II Corinthians 5:21)*
38. **An imitator of Jesus** *(Ephesians 5:1)*
39. **The Light of the World** *(Matthew 5:14)*

You have to speak the WORD also. I have 12 things that you can start with, to speak the WORD.

SPEAK THE WORD

NEVER AGAIN will I confess "I can't" for "I can do all things through Christ which strengtheneth me" (Phil. 4:13)

NEVER AGAIN will I confess lack, for "My God shall supply all or my need according to His riches in glory by Christ Jesus" (Phil. 4:19)

NEVER AGAIN will I confess fear, for "God hath not given me the spirit of fear, but of power, and of love, and of a sound mind" (2 Tim. 1:7)

NEVER AGAIN will I confess doubt and lack of faith, for "God hath given to every man the measure of faith" (Rom. 12:3)

NEVER AGAIN will I confess weakness, for "The Lord Is the strength of my life" (Psa. 27:1), and "The people that do know their God shall be strong, and do exploits" (Dan. 11:32)

NEVER AGAIN will I confess supremacy of Satan over my life, for "Greater is He that is within me, than he that is in the world" (1 Jn. 4:4)

NEVER AGAIN will I confess defeat, for "God always causeth me to triumph in Christ Jesus" (2 Cor. 2:14)

NEVER AGAIN will I confess lack of wisdom, for "Christ Jesus is made unto me wisdom from God" (1 Cor. 1:30)

NEVER AGAIN will I confess sickness, for "With His stripes I am healed"

(Isa. 53:5) and Jesus "Himself took my Infirmities and bare my sicknesses" (Mtt. 8:17)

NEVER AGAIN will I confess worries and frustrations, for I am "Casting all my cares upon Him who careth for me" (1 Pet. 5:7). In Christ, I am "care-free!"

NEVER AGAIN will I confess bondage, for "Where the spirit of the Lord is, there is liberty" (2 Cor. 3:17). My body is the temple of the Holy Spirit?

NEVER AGAIN will I confess condemnation, for "there is therefore now no condemnation to them which are in Christ-Jesus" (Rom. 8:1). I am in Christ; therefore, I am free from condemnation.

I also have 16 more that God has the answers for:
>>
>>Subject: God has the answers
>>
>>
>>>>For all the negative things we have to say to ourselves, God has a
>>>>positive
>>>>answer for it.
>>>>>
>>>>>You say: "It's impossible"
>>>>>God says: All things are possible (Luke 18:27)
>>>>>
>>>>>You say: "I'm too tired"
>>>>>God says: I will give you rest (Matthew 11:28-30)
>>>>>
>>>>>You say: "Nobody really loves me"
>>>>>God says: I love you (John 3:16 & John 13:34)
>>>>>
>>>>>You say: "I can't go on"
>>>>>God says: My grace is sufficient (II Corinthians 12:9 &
>>>>>Psalm 91:15)
>>>>>
>>>>>You say: "I can't figure things out"
>>>>>God says: I will direct your steps (Proverbs 3:5-6)
>>>>>
>>>>>You say: "I can't do it"
>>>>>God says: You can do all things (Philippians 4:13)
>>>>>
>>>>>You say: "I'm not able"
>>>>>God says: I am able (II Corinthians 9:8)
>>>>>
>>>>>You say: "It's not worth it"
>>>>>God says: It will be worth it (Roman 8:28)
>>>>>
>>>>>You say: "I can't forgive myself"

>>>>>God says: I forgive you (I John 1:9 & Romans 8:1)
>>>>>
>>>>>You say: "I can't manage"
>>>>>God says: I will supply all your needs (Philippians 4:19)
>>>>>
>>>>>You say: "I'm afraid"
>>>>>God says: I have not given you a spirit of fear (II Timothy 1:7)
>>>>>
>>>>>You say: "I'm always worried and frustrated"
>>>>>God says: Cast all your cares on ME (I Peter 5:7)
>>>>>
>>>>>You say: "I don't have enough faith"
>>>>>God says: I've given everyone a measure of faith (Romans 12:3)
>>>>>
>>>>>You say: "I'm not smart enough"
>>>>>God says: I give you wisdom (I Corinthians 1:30)
>>>>>
>>>>>You say: "I feel all alone"
>>>>>God says: I will never leave you or forsake you (Hebrews 13:5)
>>>>>
>>>>>Pass this on, you never know whose life may be in need
>>>>>of this today
>>>>>
>>>>>I AM too blessed to be stressed!"
>>>>>
>>>>>The shortest distance between a problem and a solution
>>>>>is the distance between your knees and the floor.
>>>>>
>>>>>The one who kneels to the Lord can stand up to anything.
>>>>>Love and peace be with you forever, Amen.
>>>>>
>>>>
>>>>
>>>
>>>

I AM THE RIGHTEOUSNESS OF GOD
Confession

I am the righteousness of God therefore: (•means repeat this phrase)

- Whatever I bind on earth is bond in heaven and whatever I loose on earth is loosed in heaven. (Matt. 16:19)
- I speak to mountains, "be removed and cast into the sea," believing that what I say will be done. (Mark 11:23)
- These signs follow my believing: I cast out demons, I speak in new tongues, I take up serpents, If I drink anything deadly it won't hurt me, I lay my hands on the sick and they recover. (Mark 16:17, 18)
- The Spirit of the Lord is upon me, because He has anointed me to preach the gospel to the poor; He has sent Me to heal the brokenhearted, to proclaim liberty to the captives and recovery of sight to the blind, To set at liberty those who are oppressed; To proclaim the acceptable year of the Lord. (Luke 4:18)
- I have power and authority over all demons, and to cure diseases. (Luke 9:1)
- The works that He did I will do also; and even greater works (John 14:12)
- The Spirit of truth dwells with me and is in me. (John 14:17)
- I abide in Him, and His words abide in me, I ask what I will and it is done unto me. (John 15:7)
- His joy remains in me and my joy is full. (John 15:11)
- I am one with the Father even as Jesus is one with the Father. (John 17:22)
- I cannot help but speak the things which I have seen and heard. (Acts 4:20)
- I live and move and have my being, for I am His offspring. (Acts 17:28)

- Special miracles are wrought through my hands. (Acts 19:11)
- I am justified by faith and I have peace with God through Jesus Christ.
(Rom. 5:1)
- I have access by faith into His grace where I stand and rejoice in hope.
(Rom. 5:2)
- I walk in the newness of life. (Rom. 6:4)
- I am in the likeness of Christ's resurrection. (Rom. 6:5)
- The Spirit that raised Jesus up from the dead dwells in me, and quickens my body. (Rom. 8:11)
- His Spirit beareth witness with my spirit that Iam a child of God. (Rom. 8:16)
- I am more than a conqueror through His love for me. (Rom.8:37)
- I minister in demonstration of the Spirit and power. (1 Cor. 2:4)
- I have been given the spirit of God that I might know the things that God has given me. (1 Cor. 2:12)
- I have the mind of Christ. (1 Cor.2:16)
- I am God's co-worker, I am God's garden, and I am God's building.
(1 Cor. 3:9)
- I am the temple of God and His Spirit dwells within me. (1 Cor. 3:16)
- I posess and operate in all the gifts of the Spirit. (1 Cor. 12)
- I bear the image of the heavenly. (1 Cor. 15:49)
- I am not ignorant of Satan's devices lest he should get an advantage of me.
(2 Cor. 2:11)
- I am unto God a sweet savoir of Christ. (2 Cor. 2:15)

World to be crucified and to shed his blood for our sin's. "Praise the Lord." With these thoughts in mind we should patiently endure suffering, and even rejoice that we are counted worthy to suffer for Christ's cause, remembering, "God who will not suffer you to be tempted above that ye are 'able; but will with the temptation also make a way to escape, that ye may be able to bear it." (I Cor. 10:13)

DISCOURAGEMENT
This is the Devil's best tool. Our best defense against a deceiving, lying devil is to simply believe God's Word and the precious promises it contains for us personally. "But the Lord is faithful who shall establish you, and keep you from evil" (II Thess 3:3)

SIGNS OF THE LAST DAYS AND THE SECOND COMING OF CHRIST
Nation shall rise against nation, kingdom against kingdom. (Matt. 24:7)
Earthquakes, Famines and Pestilence. (Matt. 24:7)
Men shall run to and fro, (Dan. 12:4)
Knowledge shall be increased. (Dan. 12:4)
Wars and rumors of wars. (Matt. 24:6)
Evil men shall wax worse and worse (II Tim. 3:13)
As in the days of Noah. (Matt. 24:37)
Restaurants and Taverns. (Matt. 24:49)
Falling away from faith. (I Tim. 4:1-2)
Will not endure sound doctrine (II Tim. 4:2-4)
Scoffers who don't care to hear of the second coming of Christ. (II Peter 3:3-14)
Thy shall say peace and safety (I Thess 5:1-3)
Men walking after their own lusts. (Jude ?:16-18)
Heaping treasures for last days. (James 5:3-6)
False Preachers. (Matt. 24:11)
Men and horses out of work (Zech. 8:10)

Automobiles (Nahum 2:3-4)

Air ships (Isaiah 31:5 & 60:8)

Perilous times (II Tim. 3:1)

Disobedient to parents (II Tim. 3:2)

Lovers of pleasures more than lovers of God, having a form of Godliness, but denying the power thereof (II Tim. 3:4-5)

Jews returning to Palestine (Jer. 32:36-42)

Coming world Dictator (II Thess. 2:1-4 & Rev. 13:?)

Length of his rule (Rev. 13:5)

Some will worship him. (Rev. 13:8)

Doom to those that worship him. (Rev. 14:9-11)

Picture of last war. (Dan. 12:1 & Matt. 24:21 & 27, Jer. 25:29-30, Mark 13:10)

By their fruits ye shall know them. (Matt. 7:20)

THE BEATITUDES

From Christs sermon on the Mount

Blessed are the poor in spirit: for theirs is the kingdom of heaven.

Blessed are they that mourn: for they shall be comforted.

Blessed are meek: for they shall inherit the earth.

Blessed are they which do hunger and thirst after righteousness: for they shall be filled.

Blessed are the merciful: for they shall obtain mercy.

Blessed are the pure in heart: for they shall see God.

Blessed are the peacemakers: for they shall be called the children of God.

Blessed are they which are persecuted for righteousness' sake: for theirs is the kingdom of heaven.

Blessed are ye, when men revile you, and persecute you, and shall say all manner of evil against you falsely, for my sake. (Matt. 5:1-13)

Epilogue

A lot has happened in my life...some bad, some good. You might think I should still have bitterness, hatred and anger in my heart. My old man, before I met Jesus, did. But, the new man is free from those things. As 2 Cor. 5:17 says,

"Therefore if any man is in Christ, {he is} a new creature; the old things passed away; behold, new things have come." (NAS)

My dad passed away and before he died, there were some Christians at his apartment standing in a circle holding hands and praying. My dad accepted Jesus Christ as his Lord and Savior and asked for forgiveness of his sins. This was about a month before he passed away.

Mom accepted Jesus Christ as the Lord and Savior of her life and also asked forgiveness for her sins. Mom prayed for us kids to get saved. I'm an answer to her prayers. There's power in prayer, so don't ever stop praying for your loved ones.

I got to witness to my friend and say the sinner's prayer with him for his salvation.

I remember one time I went to the doctor because I was sick and he prescribed some medicine with sulfa in it. It turned out, I was allergic to sulfa. I broke out in a rash and I could hardly walk. I remember crawling on my hands and knees to bed, moaning and groaning because my legs hurt so bad. I had my eyes on the pain instead of Jesus. All of the sudden, I started praying, thanking Jesus for the healing, praising Him, singing, lifting my hands up to Him, and laughing. I was in the presence of the Lord and the Holy Spirit healed my legs. Praise God! The doctor said if I even took sulfa again, I could lose my life, or be in a wheel chair for life. Thank you, Jesus.

Another time, I got pneumonia and lost hearing in both ears. I had them lay hands on me at church and pray for me. I was healed, and got 80% of my hearing back. Praise God!

I got a card from someone at work once that said, "... thanks for being there when I needed someone to talk to and thanks for your prayers."

We got a card from a friend that came out and stayed with us on her vacation. While she was here, her best friend had a heart attack and was in the hospital for three days in the Intensive Care Unit. Before I went to work, I held hands with my wife and her friend, and we prayed for her healing. Here's what she wrote to us. "Thank you so much for all your prayers, good thoughts, and the angel magnet. I know for a fact that without everyone's prayers I would not be here today. Love, Joyce"

My sister wrote, "I'm very proud to be your sister, through all the hard times, you've turned out great. I don't say it much, but I love you lots! Love, your Sister" Thank you, Jesus.

My oldest son wrote, "I treated you like dirt and I'm so sorry for that. You never did anything to me for me to treat you that way and I'm sorry!!! I know that I'm different looking than your other friends, like my hair, earrings and tattoos. I don't know if you would want to be seen with me though. The old saying goes, Don't judge someone by their appearance. I'm thankful for all that you have done for me. I know that I can't take back what I've done, but I hope I can be forgiven." We did forgive him and I'm happy that we are talking again. Thank you for giving me the chance to explain my story to you. Thank you, Jesus.

This card I saved for last.

Dear Son,

You almost did away with yourself, and I prayed for you and you gave yourself to the Lord. I'm so proud to see the Lord work in your life and to give you a wife like Karen. Isn't the Lord so wonderful the way He works in our lives? P.S. And to see what He has done in Karen's life also. Love you, too, Karen. Love you, Son, and God bless you. God be with you always, Mother

My mom went to be with the Lord on May 20, 1999. We found this card and my Mom wrote this to be for my birthday back in 1986. Thank you Lord for my mother and her prayers.

There are many, many more I could write, but I just wanted you to see as you read the book that Jesus is real and He is alive today, and He can forgive you, save you, and change your life around for the better.

A lot has happened in my life...some bad, some good. You might think I should still have bitterness, hatred and anger in my heart. My old man, before I met Jesus, did. But, the new man is free from those things. As 2 Cor. 5:17 says,

"Therefore if any man is in Christ, {he is} a new creature; the old things passed away; behold, new things have come." (NAS)

All things are new and life without Jesus just wouldn't be worth living. If it wasn't for Jesus, I wouldn't be the man I am now. I wouldn't love and care for others, and I wouldn't feel sad for others, want to help them out, share my story. I'd still be living in all of my sins.

As Matthew 9:26 says, "And looking upon {them} Jesus said to them, "With men this is impossible, but with God all things are possible." (NAS)

So I don't just depend on myself, I just give everything to Jesus to take care of me and everyone and everything else in my life. When I pray, I do believe that I will receive and I will.

Matthew 21:22 says, "And all things you ask in prayer, believing, you shall receive." (NAS)

I don't want anyone to be upset or angry with me for telling my story to help others and to testify of the Lord and to share what Jesus has done for me. I know that I can't please everyone and I'd rather have man disown me than God.

I pray that the Holy Spirit will minister to you as you read this book and the scriptures I've included. And I pray you'll invite Him into your heart and life.

Matt 10:28 "And do not fear those who kill the body, but are unable to kill the soul; but rather fear Him who is able to destroy both soul and body in hell."

(NAS)

John 14:6 "Jesus said to him, "I am the way, and the truth, and the life; no one comes to the Father, but through Me." (NAS)

Jesus also said in John 8:32 "and you shall know the truth, and the truth shall make you free." (NAS)

I'm thankful I found the truth and am truly free. My old man listened to the lies of the devil and his tricks and he cheated me out of everything God had for me. But, God loved me so much, He waited for me to turn my life over to Him, so He could take care of me. God never left me alone or gave up on me and He won't give up on you either. All you have to do is accept Him, turn your life over to Him, and He will take care of you. Whoever comes to Jesus after reading this book will then be lead by the Spirit.

John 12:32 "And I, if I be lifted up from the earth, will draw all men to Myself."

I don't have to do anything but tell you about Jesus and He'll do the rest.

As you know, I've been divorced twice. Deut 24:1 'When a man takes a wife and marries her, and it happens that she finds no favor in his eyes because he has found some indecency in her, and he writes her a certificate of divorce and puts {it} in her hand and sends her out from his house," (NAS)

Matt 19:9 "And I say to you, whoever divorces his wife, except for immorality, and marries another woman commits adultery." (NAS)

My first two marriages were when I was still in my sin and not living for God. I didn't even know God then. I was heading for hell and everything I was doing in my life pointed me in that direction. I don't blame either of my first two wives for leaving, but that's all been forgiven because I accepted Jesus.

Now, I'm a Christian and I have a Christian wife. Life has more meaning for me now than ever before and I have the promise of eternal life with my Lord and Savior, Jesus Christ.

This book is to glorify my Jesus. Pray, talk and listen... there's hope for you!

Write or call:
Ray & Karen Berto   (253) 922-7773
c/o Faith Family Church
1702 Milton Way
Milton, WA 98354
Ray & Karen Berto
P.O. Box 748
Sumner, WA 98390
Prayer Line: (253) 863-3033
E-mail: rberto@comcast.net
Website: http://www.lighthouserm.com

Become a Part of the Lighthouse Rescuer Ministry

Luke 6:38 says "Give, and it will be given to you; good measure, pressed down, shaken together, running over, they will pour into your lap. For by your standard of measure it will be measured to you in return." (NAS)

I'm going to let the Holy Spirit speak to your hearts if you'd like to be part of this ministry. If you'd like to become a part of Lighthouse Rescuer Ministry. My plan is to make this book available to anyone who wants it and needs it... This book is a tool to win others for Jesus and help them to know God.

But we would still like to ask you to pray for this ministry, that God will bless it and use it.

Thank you.

Thanks

I want to thank these people for helping me with my book. Thanks to Peggy Chambers, Judy Walker and last, but certainly not least, my wife Karen.

I pray for God's blessing on all of them. I'm glad God brought all these Christian people into my life. I want to say a special thanks to Susan Fox for her part in this book, because the final wouldn't have been possible without her.

I am thankful for all of the events that happened in my life and the people in my life – my sister, my mom, my kids and most of all, Jesus.

God Bless!

Yours in Christ's Love,
Brother Ray

CPSIA information can be obtained at www.ICGtesting.com
Printed in the USA
BVOW041204210911

271770BV00001B/154/P